Hold me close

Kiralee Standing

Presentation by *BookLeaf Publishing*

Web: www.bookleafpub.com

E-mail: info@bookleafpub.com

ISBN: 978-93-95784-22-1

First edition 2022

DEDICATION

I dedicate this work to others like me who struggle or who have struggled with mental illness, suicidal thoughts and/or suicide attempts. I am grateful for my family and friends who have stood by me and validated my feelings and dreams.

#1

I always wonder why I am drawn to the darkness

For the stars provide a cascade of feelings

That I cannot comprehend alone

Your embracing arms

Reach for the part of me that you knew first

The girl who could once manage her emotions

Is drawn to the curiosity and danger of the night

You may think of that as weakness

But facing its extremities is easier than

Being burdened by a repeated bottling

And trapping of emotions

How do you hold yourself

When everything you have ever known

And everyone you have ever loved

Becomes momentarily estranged and seemingly
guarded from you?

They try to tell you death is the answer

But the glistening stars

Are a begging of self-forgiveness

You are not the things and people

That took your very innocence

You are the person that looks out for others

That loves deeply and wholeheartedly

Even when your own mind is scattered

Anything to delay the inevitable cyclical
emotional rollercoaster

That hits and drowns you every night

While feeling like every living moment you are
further slipping into the depths

Of nothingness and worthlessness

The love you give feels unreciprocated and
pointless

But then you realise that's what they are trying
to poison you with

And you come to trust its voice more than your
own

For it has been there in every downfall and every
moment of crisis

To attempt to guide you towards an end that isn't
written for you yet

That's when help is necessary to control it

To guide your mind towards the reasons for
living

Rather than the reasons to not

Entering that office felt unnatural

Like I was cheating those who love me most

By needing help to manage the voices

Telling me I was better off dead than alive

But by embracing them more

The further your loved ones appear to vanish

For you were not a mistake

You were a traumatised young girl

Hoping and waiting for her chance to

Bloom

#2

When I first open my eyes to face yet another
day

I realise that I am nowhere near where I intend
to be heading

The thought of being behind in life constantly
haunts me

Unsettling me to my core

But yet I have come to understand

That in order to move forward

I have to face it and deconstruct it

To understand its illogical stance

To face the things that cyclically hold me
hostage

For healing needs to be addressed with
vulnerability and risk of relapse

Not an unrelenting sense of urgency

Loving hard and seemingly unrequitable doesn't
make you unlovable

It makes you feel isolated and unreachable

Loving hard doesn't make you weak

It brings another reason to speak out

Rather than continue to hold within

My strength lies in the belief that I am worthy

We are all worthy of justice and redemption

But society only sees and shines light

On what it can benefit from

But we are just suicidal people

Less important than those presenting with a
broken arm

While our souls are broken

#3

Have you ever wanted to escape and be forgotten?

Even if it's only temporary

But I don't want to be forgotten

I want to be remembered

While being able to forget

Your refreshing soul reminded me

That I am worth more than my past

Our shy walks in the park and surrounding streets

Have brought us to this very moment

Our love adds up to more than

We could ever imagine

When the accident happened

You held me closer

Reminding me of my worthiness

My right to love

And be loved

The storms seem to last forever

But your strength

My dear

Challenges my fear of expression

The fear of feeling

Is no more

Your eyes envelop me

Take my hand

And let me show you

The love you have always deserved

Body to body

Soul to soul

Our embrace an endless harmony

Of words that I have kept within

You don't have to hide anymore

All the Gods

All the heavens

All the hells

Are within you

Greets me every morning

Your love is like a song

I listen to on repeat

A soulmate and best friend in one

Souls connected

Being seen is better than hiding

Being open is better than drowning

Together or apart

Don't forget my love

That you are a masterpiece

But everyone won't understand you

For some scars are mistaken as flaws

You are more than that

Your beauty lies much deeper than

The merely physical

It lays in the knowing

That you behold the power

To heal from the previously unspoken

The longing for better days

Are no more

Help me to help you

Understand your grief

Is not to be feared

It doesn't have to control you

Take my hand

And soar with me into

A place of forgiveness

Let it take over you

To allow yourself to truly

Heal

#4

If I am so weak and selfish

What does that make you?

You have held me hostage for years

Taking away what's left of the real me

But I don't feel real without you

I don't feel balanced without you

That domineering yet comforting voice

Wills me into another dimension

Was I weak when he held me down?

Was I weak when I shut my eyes?

Was I weak when I didn't cry?

But where's the evidence?

Are you sure he even touched you?

Maybe you had a nightmare?

A living nightmare

Sure!

He touched me!

He violated me!

He was supposed to love me!

And I didn't feel loved

There is nothing poetic about that

Your voice gave me further reason to

Understand this as misguided love

Rather than what it really was

RAPE

Did I give you the satisfaction?

Holding me down while drowning my mind

Into believing this was normal

I hear you and see you

Everywhere

You're gone but still remain

Leave me alone!

You warped what love is to me

While your hands explored deeper

My mind wandered

If a boy likes you…

No!

He would not touch you

He would not strip away your innocence

He would not violate you

He would respect you and earn your trust

If he were properly educated

No more excuses!

I am a victim of many things

From the touch of your dirty hands

I am a victim to my own mind

But simultaneously a warrior fighting daily battles

What about our little secret?

You may have asked me with pleading eyes

I was a child!

I misunderstood your abuse as love

Love is love

But this wasn't out of love

It was out of manipulation

I already felt so small and lost

Is that why I am so self-destructive and
ultimately seek nothingness?

You signed everything "with love"

Why not "with abuse"?

Did you read my letter?

Did it break you down to your core?

Until you return again

With anguish

Goodbye

#5

When my mind drifts from safety to danger

I struggle to find the words to simply express my anguish.

It's like my mind and body become disconnected

And I cannot tell the difference between

A loving hand and a blade passing across my skin

For how can a person feel so much?

That in one moment I glimpse into a manifestation of a future worth living

My mind draws in on every bad thing I have ever done

I have never understood sin

But I am starting to think that

Every day I live is another sin

And every beautiful moment I experience

Is outweighed by the reality that as much as I try

I will never weigh up to you or who you wanted
me to be

Some say the body is a temple to be fed

But all I feel is pain and shame when I lay in bed

And awake the next morning

For how can I feel happy now

When I'm stuck and dwell on the past?

I wish I could tell you how I feel

But if I were to tell you truly

You would think differently of me

And see me as I truly am

A young woman struggling to find her way

In a world that cannot understand her

Even when I seem to have everything

There is always something missing

Something lingering that I cannot

Find the courage to free and detach myself from

It's like there's someone's breath constantly on
me

Hands constantly around my neck

Waiting for me to feel weak and vulnerable

I thought my innocence was my protector

But exactly like you

It betrayed me

It made me see and hear things

I didn't and still don't understand

You cannot help someone who doesn't want to
be saved

#6

But it's not that I don't want to be saved

I just want to be saved my reliving my worst moments

Reliving moments that I was never educated on

How a boys touch at school meant he liked me

And how when you touched me

I presumed the same principle

If he gives you attention

He likes you

If he hits you

He likes you

When he lifted my school dress up

That was out of love

But now I realise it was

Manipulation

I was innocent and I was an easy target

It was our little secret

And even now I cannot find myself to be able to

Bring the appropriate words together

To tell them

To cry out to them

That I suffered and am still suffering

What if the suffering never ends?

What if I deserved it?

Is that why when my clothes begin to fall onto
the floor

I'm drawn back to those moments

When I was still innocent and untouched

And pure

I've thought about seeking out religion

But I don't and never will understand it

So for now

I will continue to bury myself

In the remnants of who I used to be

And the person I could have been

If your dirty and wrinkled hands

Hadn't stripped me of my purity

All I wanted was to be loved and worthy

But you objectified me beyond what was right

Even though it is also wrong

I wonder how your desire and gratification

Was worth more than loving me like you should
have

You cannot touch me ever again

But there is still a deep ache in my soul of all
that has been

Lost

#7

If I became hollow and intangible

Would you call out to me?

If I were bruised and hurt

Would you reach out your hand?

If I were damaged and beyond fixing

Would you fight for me?

But what do you think I mean?

My arms and legs are not compromised

There lies no pain

Then why did you call us all here for?

You are not dying!

But I am!

My eyes flood and flow

Like an endless tumult

But why can't you make it stop?

You are in control

But I am not!

I am controlled by the bad

The bad what?

The bad thoughts!

The bad impulses!

The bad memories!

Your touch is the deepest pain

But he soothes that pain

He holds me when you re-enter

My tarnished mind

He reminds me you are no longer

Existent

Then why do you continue to harm yourself?

It is both a means of coping and destruction

Don't you tell me off when

The drink is where you turn to numb

Your pain

Your dread

Your being

We all have our way

Of making it to the next day

Before you say no

Think of the last time you were truly happy

You can't remember?

Do you understand now?

#8

27

But they didn't put me here

Who am I without

Self-doubt

Self-hatred

Self-harm?

I have no one to blame

Except for myself

If I ever cried to you

Or asked for help

Forget it

All of it

Erase me from your

Memory

The tap is dripping

But for how much longer?

Does it make sense to you yet?

You tell me not to be constrained by time

But time is running out

And so am

I

Give me your hand

But please don't cry

I have cried endless oceans

Only to end up in the same place

Learn to laugh instead

Did you have a bad day?

Laugh

You aren't taking it seriously

They say

But maybe that's the problem?

Holding onto the seriousness and complexity

Drowns my soul more

Telling me I am not capable

Of being successful

Of being happy

Of being a mother

Stop trying to take the noose away

When in my mind

It is already tied

#9

When my mind returns to suicide

The light becomes unreachable

My eyes are drawn to the possibilities

The chances of a quick death

My hands are no longer just hands

They behold the power to self-destruct

If you tell me to stop

All I want to do is drift further

While my heart tells me

To let you envelop me

To let you in

Not push you further

Until I can no longer

Recognise myself

Your love is like an ocean

But while you beg me to drown in yours

I drown further in the depths of my struggle

When I was a child

They told me love was shown

Not spoken

But you do both

Your arms are my warmth

And I'm afraid to get cold

For I may stay there

And never return

Why am I like this?

I cry to you and myself some nights

But I am not as bad as those people

The people who mistook my smile for a yes

For consent

If words had been spoken

Would things have changed?

If I had turned my smile into a frown

Would I still feel so dirty now?

Have I come to hate you so much

That I hate myself too?

I always feel like I'm too much

But never enough

#10

When I was living

I didn't care what they thought

I didn't check myself

I didn't shy from interaction

Now I am in a state

Of mere survival

My breath is haunted

By this knowing

That I have limited myself

My inner strength

Is shadowed by inner doubt

Blame dominates my mind

If I had done things differently

If I paid attention to the smaller things

Maybe my mind could remember

The finer details

Of a time where I wasn't riddled

With the thought of death

A time I was close to myself

A time where tears could fall shamelessly

Now

It feels like shame follows me everywhere

Like a cold I cannot shake off

The shame of not being who I want to be

Who I dreamed to be

The shame of being objectified and sexualised

The shame of feeling

If I continue to hide

Survival is it

But if I can just hold on

And reach out to your loving hand

Maybe this nightmare

Will blossom into something bigger

Will shift my mind towards growing my roots

Rather than continuously

Tearing them down

#11

Don't hold them above yourself

Young one

You are not any less than them

You will soar and leave them behind

For your strength is stronger

Than their hatred

Stronger than anything

You are not a bird who has lost their wings

You are a bird

Afraid to lose your normalcy

But you are meant for bigger things

Bigger than your current horizon

Young one

They cannot touch you or caress you

Without your permission

If only you were taught

The difference between love and

Abuse

He is not entitled to you

Do not be afraid to hide

But don't hide the real you

You are a worthy warrior

They should have helped

Instead of ignoring the obvious

Signs of abuse

Young one

You are not to blame

Blame is not for you to hold within

For you were manipulated into passing

Abuse as love

Your hands are your hands

Your thoughts are your thoughts

But don't keep the secret

You are worthy of love

Abuse is abuse

Young one

You were supposed to be here

You are not a mistake

Don't be afraid to use your voice

Fight back

I just can't forgive myself

For still remaining quiet

For not advocating for others

That abuse isn't love

And love isn't abuse

You deserved so much better

But for now

Young one

I will fight for you

I will heal you

My inner child

This is just the beginning

#12

It's still beating

But there's an underlying struggle

Of wanting it to stop

But what envelops it?

A mother who worries deeply

A father who just wants to help

A sister who is always there

A grandmother holding on

To the knowing that she is loved

A partner who would bleed

Just to keep you safe

And shows you he is here

To stay

And the animals

They know everything

They show you love

And annoy you

When you desperately need it

You could be holding a blade

While they catch your tears

For the blade will never love you

But they always will

See what you need to see

Not what your thoughts are feeding you

Trying to sabotage any progress

Any loss of shame

Towards what you couldn't control

The hurt changed you

But it has not defeated you

Your heart is full

Of more love than hate

Your dreams are scattered

Your mind is puzzled

But while your mind tells you to let go

Your heart begs for connection

Scream it if you need

But you are so loved

So worthy

Hold on for the curiosity

Of a future unwritten

If you leave now

Your story will remain unwritten

Write the narrative you want to be remembered
by

Hold onto the fact that you are growing

You are evolving

You just need help

To heal the things

You keep distracting yourself from

I have never met a person

With linear healing or recovery

While there may be linearity in your dark
thoughts

You no longer need to hold that space alone

Please hold on

We need you on earth

Not under the earth

#13

Loneliness can be frightening

But simultaneously comforting

In those moments

My only aim is to hold on

Hold onto the belief that

You will rise again

You are loved

And never a burden

But in those darker moments

When I lose all bodily sensations

My mind tells me otherwise

You are worthless

You are unlovable

You are a burden

I know it's time to

Break the cycle

And feed the positive thoughts

As you are capable

Of greater things

Of breaking down the barriers

Of intergenerational trauma

Admonition (Part 1)

All I can hear is the tick, tick, tick.

Will it ever stop?

They will not let me be!

They will not let me see the light!

I wonder how long it will be

Until they find out

That I have managed to escape from existence

That this body is no longer mine.

A maze of conflict and obliviousness

For which I fail to grasp my surroundings.

This mind has beaten more than this heart ever
did.

The question they are all pondering is

When will she finally succumb to it?

And when will it be all that is ever remembered
of her name?

A reminder of what could have been done

Is all too familiar.

This is all an annihilation

A disaster

But drawn from a social construct.

I hear a lot of, "if only"

"What if...?"

And what lacks in the expression is recognition

That we were human just like you!

Do you understand now?

Do not try to understand!

You did not try to understand then

So do not bother 'worrying' out of your wits
now!

"I am fine."

Is that what you want me to say?

Stop expecting those words!

I cannot hide it any longer!

I remember the night quite vividly

Where my thoughts were driving me towards

The yew tree down the street.

A body and mind

That simultaneously were not

Mine.

Unconsciously

As if overcome with my demonic thoughts

A knife glided its way

Across my repeatedly severed arm.

While my skin ached with guilt

My mind urged me that it was not enough.

More! More! More!

It would never be enough.

And when the realisation washed over me

Of the act my mind had committed upon my
body

My anxious and conscious mind returned with

Hurrying thoughts and utter numbness.

Admonition (Part 2)

I can't go back there again!

You can't take me away from this place

Destruction is all I have ever known!

Get away from me!

Stop yelling at me!

Punish them!

For they are the perpetrators

The controllers

The destroyers

Not me!

You thought you had me captured

But you will never take me away again!

I must distance myself from these grotesque
thoughts and accusations.

My mind needs to be replenished

Reconstructed.

On a dark and stormy day

They took me away.

Countless months forward

On a bright summer's day

They labelled me as being a 'solved case'

Forcing me to re-enter this blasphemous society.

They said that I could last if I tried

But what they failed to grasp was

The more I try

The more I feel outside of my own skin.

You cannot cure me!

Do not even try

For you already know what I am capable of.

And I am not afraid to do it again!

But this time

I will make sure it is a success!

#16

Loneliness can be frightening

But simultaneously comforting.

In those moments

My only aim is to hold on.

Hold onto the belief that

You will rise again

You are loved

And never a burden.

But in those darker moments

When I lose all bodily sensations

My mind tells me otherwise.

You are worthless

You are unlovable

You are a burden.

I know it's time to

Break the cycle

And feed the positive thoughts.

As you are capable

Of greater things.

Of breaking down the barriers

Of intergenerational trauma.

#17

When I lose myself

Death seemingly becomes the only possibility

But now I understand this is a trauma response.

While death may seem easier than facing myself

He continues to remind me

That my pain

Becomes their pain.

I am not like an eraser

My physical existence is not erased by my
breath stopping.

Instead

Those who loved me

Will continue to see me in places

And people they meet.

But when I want to jump into unknown waters

I do not care of their anguish.

For my anguish is indescribable.

But I wish I could tell you

How much I love you.

My chest tightens

And the words don't flow like they should.

I am scared

Of revealing too much

Of scaring you off.

I will keep trying

For your happiness is worth the pain.

#18

You can't see me

But I'm here.

In the back of your mind

I seek your pain.

I take away all of your happiness

And replace it

With pure sadness.

It's okay

You don't need to thank me

This is my job.

To make your life

Miserable.

You take your pills

But I'm still there

In the back of your mind

Ready to pounce

At any time